CALUMET CITY PUBLIC LIBRARY

3 1613 00496 7124

W9-BZB-726

TO THE RESCUE!

Firefighters
to the Rescue
Around the World

Linda Staniford

J
628.9
STA

Capstone $17⁹⁴ 03/16

CALUMET CITY
PUBLIC LIBRARY

capstone

© 2016 Heinemann-Raintree
an imprint of Capstone Global Library, LLC
Chicago, Illinois

To contact Capstone Global Library please call 800-747-4992, or visit our web site www.capstonepub.com

All rights reserved. No part of this publication may be reproduced or transmitted in any form or by any means, electronic or mechanical, including photocopying, recording, taping, or any information storage and retrieval system, without permission in writing from the publisher.

Edited by Linda Staniford
Designed by Steve Mead
Picture research by Eric Gohl
Production by Aileen Taylor
Originated by Capstone Global Library Ltd
Printed and bound in China

20 19 18 17 16
10 9 8 7 6 5 4 3 2 1

Library of Congress Cataloging-in-Publication Data
Cataloging-in-publication information is on file with the Library of Congress.
Written by Linda Staniford
ISBN 978-1-4846-2751-8 (hardcover)
ISBN 978-1-4846-2755-6 (paperback)
ISBN 978-1-4846-2759-4 (eBook PDF)

Acknowledgments
The author and publisher are grateful to the following for permission to reproduce copyright material:
Alamy: Ace Stock Limited, 7, Ian Marlow, 13, 22 (top), John Joannides, 20, Mia Caruana, 6; AP Photo: The Yomiuri Shimbun, 5; Getty Images: Christopher Furlong, 19, Corpo Nazionale dei Vigili del Fuoco, 17, Orlando Sierra, 18, Stringer/STR, 15; iStockphoto: erlucho, 10, Graffizone, back cover (right), 12, omgimages, 21, slobo, back cover (left), 8; Newscom: Broker/olf image, 9, 22 (middle), Xinhua News Agency/Country Fire Authority, 14, 22 (bottom), Xinhua News Agency/Zhang Jia, 11; Shutterstock: art-pho, cover (bottom), Jerry Sharp, 4, Ververidis Vasilis, cover (top); U.S. Coast Guard: 16

Design Elements: Shutterstock

Every effort has been made to contact copyright holders of any material reproduced in this book. Any omissions will be rectified in subsequent printings if notice is given to the publisher.

All the Internet addresses (URLs) given in this book were valid at the time of going to press. However, due to the dynamic nature of the Internet, some addresses may have changed, or sites may have changed or ceased to exist since publication. While the author and publisher regret any inconvenience this may cause readers, no responsibility for any such changes can be accepted by either the author or the publisher.

007501RRDS16

Contents

Some words are shown in bold, **like this**. You can find out what they mean by looking in the glossary.

How Do Firefighters Help Us?

Firefighters are always ready to rush to the rescue. When a fire starts, they work hard to put it out as quickly as they can.

Firefighters also deal with other kinds of emergencies all over the world. For example, they rescue people trapped in cars or in floods.

What Do Firefighters Wear?

A firefighter wears a **waterproof** jacket and boots. They are made of **fireproof** material that will not melt in the heat of a fire.

Firefighters also wear helmets to protect their heads. The helmet has a **visor**. It protects the firefighter's face from the heat.

How Do Firefighters Travel?

A fire engine carries firefighters and their equipment to a burning building. Fire engines are brightly colored. They have a flashing light and a loud **siren**.

In Venice, Italy, people travel on **canals** instead of roads, so firefighters use boats to get to fires. Other firefighters use motorcycles to reach fires quickly.

What Equipment Do Firefighters Use?

Fire engines carry some water in tanks, but they also have very long hoses. These can be connected to fire **hydrants** to pump water onto the fire.

hydrant

Fire engines also have long ladders on the roof. Firefighters use these to climb up high buildings to rescue people from inside the buildings.

What Else Do Firefighters Carry?

Axes and rams are used to get into locked buildings to rescue people. Fire **extinguishers** help put out special kinds of fires, such as electrical fires.

After a traffic accident, firefighters help rescue people trapped in their cars. They use gas torches to cut the metal.

3 1613 00496 7124

CALUMET CITY PUBLIC LIBRARY

What Types of Fire Are There?

In Australia, it can be very hot and dry. **Bush fires** can spread very quickly. Firefighters use helicopters to spray water onto the fire to control it.

Special teams of firefighters deal with fires at airports. Planes carry a lot of fuel, which can burn very quickly if it catches fire.

How Do Firefighters Save Lives at Sea?

Oil rig fires are very **dangerous** because all the oil nearby keeps them burning. Firefighters on boats spray seawater at the fires for a long time to put them out.

Firefighters can rescue people who are trapped on a boat that is sinking. They have special equipment to cut through the side of the boat so that they can bring the trapped people out to safety.

How Else Do Firefighters Rescue People?

When there is an earthquake, buildings may **collapse**. Firefighters can rescue people who are trapped underneath the **rubble**.

When there is a flood, people may get trapped upstairs in their houses or on the roof. Firefighters use boats to get to them and take them to dry land.

Making the World a Safer Place!

Firefighters often visit schools and communities. They show people what to do if something catches fire in their home.

Firefighters are very brave people. It is good to know we can call them if there is a fire. But it is also important to know how to stay safe near fires.

Quiz

What have you learned about firefighters around the world?

Question 1

What are gas torches used for?
a) to give light
b) to put out fires
c) to cut metal so that people trapped inside cars can be rescued

Question 2

What kind of transportation do firefighters use in Venice?
a) boats
b) motorcycles
c) bicycles

Question 3

How do firefighters put out bush fires in Australia?
a) using fire extinguishers
b) by spraying water from helicopters
c) by climbing ladders

Answers: 1 c), 2 a), 3 b)

22

Glossary

bush fire fire in the countryside where the grass and bushes burn very fast

canal human-made waterway

collapse fall down suddenly; buildings often collapse during earthquakes

dangerous likely to cause harm or injury

extinguisher device with water and chemicals inside it that is used to put out fires

fireproof does not burn

hydrant large, upright pipe with a valve that draws water from the city's water supply. Hydrants supply water for fighting fires.

rubble broken bricks and other material left from a building that has fallen down or been demolished

siren device that makes a loud sound

visor covering, often attached to a hat or helmet, designed to shade the eyes

waterproof able to keep water out

Find Out More

Books

Chancellor, Deborah. *Fire Rescue* (Emergency Vehicles). Mankato, Minn.: Smart Apple Media, 2014.

Royston, Angela. *Diary of a Firefighter* (Heinemann First Library). Chicago: Heinemann Library, 2014.

Internet sites

Facthound offers a safe, fun way to find Internet sites related to this book. All of the sites on Facthound have been researched by our staff.

Here's all you do:
Visit www.facthound.com
Type in this code: 9781484627518

Index